CORE LIBRARY OF US STATES

MICHIGAN

BY JANE VERNON

CONTENT CONSULTANT
Cara Shelly
Department of History
Oakland University

Core Library
An Imprint of Abdo Publishing
abdobooks.com

abdobooks.com

Published by Abdo Publishing, a division of ABDO, PO Box 398166, Minneapolis, Minnesota 55439.

Printed in the United States of America, North Mankato, Minnesota.
052022
092022

Cover Photo: Shutterstock Images
Interior Photos: Alexey Stiop/Shutterstock Images, 4–5, 43; Red Line Editorial, 7 (Michigan), 7 (USA); North Wind Picture Archives/Alamy, 10–11; Frederic Remington/Sarin Images/Granger Historical Picture Archive, 14; Shutterstock Images, 16 (flag); iStockphoto, 16 (bird), 16 (fish), 16 (flower), 20; Jay Ondreicka/Shutterstock Images, 16 (turtle); Shriram Patki/iStockphoto, 22–23; Robert Chao/ Shutterstock Images, 24; John McCormick/Shutterstock Images, 27, 45; World History Archive/ Alamy, 30–31; B. S. Pollard/iStockphoto, 33; Gilles Petard/Redferns/Getty Images, 36–37; Steven King/Icon Sportswire/AP Images, 40; Yochika Photographer/Shutterstock Images, 41

Editor: Angela Lim
Series Designer: Joshua Olson

Library of Congress Control Number: 2021951388

Publisher's Cataloging-in-Publication Data

Names: Vernon, Jane, author.
Title: Michigan / by Jane Vernon
Description: Minneapolis, Minnesota : Abdo Publishing, 2023 | Series: Core library of US states | Includes online resources and index.
Identifiers: ISBN 9781532197635 (lib. bdg.) | ISBN 9781098270391 (ebook)
Subjects: LCSH: U.S. states--Juvenile literature. | Midwest States--Juvenile literature. | Michigan--History--Juvenile literature. | Physical geography--United States--Juvenile literature.
Classification: DDC 977.4--dc23

Population demographics broken down by race and ethnicity come from the 2019 census estimate. Population totals come from the 2020 census.

CONTENTS

SEABISCUIT CAFÉ
Ryba's Fudge Shops
To Bead Or Not To Bead

THE GREAT LAKES STATE

Tourists step off the ferry and onto the dock of Mackinac (pronounced MACK-in-aw) Island. They feel as though they have traveled back in time. Cars are not allowed on the island. Instead of automobile traffic, the visitors hear the gentle clip-clop of horses' hooves. The horses pull carriages through the old-fashioned town. Tourists on bicycles pedal along at a relaxed pace. Behind the rows of colorful

People ride on bikes through Mackinac Island's downtown.

Victorian-style buildings, the lush green leaves of a thick grove of trees flutter in the breeze.

PERSPECTIVES

WHY NO CARS ON MACKINAC ISLAND?

Mackinac Island was once the center of the Great Lakes fur trade and was also home to a military outpost. People heard about the beauty of the island, and it became a popular place to visit. Tour guides used horse-drawn carriages to show visitors beautiful sites around the island in the late 1800s. When people brought the first automobiles to the island, the carriage drivers asked the village council to ban cars because the noise was scaring their horses. The leaders agreed, and the ban is still in place to this day.

Mackinac Island is located in Lake Huron, one of the four Great Lakes that border Michigan. The other three are Lakes Superior, Michigan, and Erie. Michigan borders the most Great Lakes of any state. This is why the state is nicknamed the Great Lakes State.

ABOUT MICHIGAN

Michigan is part of the Midwest region of the United States.

MAP OF MICHIGAN

Michigan's unique shape allows it to touch many of the Great Lakes. How does this map help you understand the state's connection to different waterways?

SOO LOCKS

The Soo Locks make travel between the Great Lakes possible. The canal system connects Lake Superior and Lake Huron. There is a height difference of 21 feet (6 m) between the two lakes. Boats can be lifted or lowered by slowly filling or draining the locks.

The state is made up of two pieces of land. The Upper Peninsula (UP) lies to the north. It connects to Wisconsin in the west. Lakes Superior, Huron, and Michigan surround it to the north, east, and south. The Lower Peninsula extends north from Indiana and Ohio. Lakes Michigan, Huron, and Erie all touch it. The Lower Peninsula also borders Canada in the east. Michigan has more than 3,000 miles (4,800 km) of freshwater shoreline, the most of any US state.

In 1923 drivers could travel between the peninsulas only by ferry. The Mackinac Bridge opened for traffic in 1957. At the time, it was the longest suspension bridge in the world. The bridge spans 5 miles (8 km).

Michigan's Lower Peninsula is shaped like a mitten. The state's most-populated cities are found in the Lower Peninsula. The two largest are Detroit and Grand Rapids. Lansing is located in between these two cities. It is the capital.

Tourists and Michiganders alike visit sports stadiums and art museums in the cities. The state's natural beauty also draws many visitors each year. Forests cover large areas of the UP. Tourists enjoy hiking, fishing, and camping in state parks. They visit small cities, such as Traverse City and Marquette. These lakeside locations blend city life with outdoor adventures.

EXPLORE ONLINE

Chapter One talks about the Great Lakes. The article at the website below goes into more depth on this topic. How is the information from the website the same as the information in Chapter One? What new information did you learn from the website?

THE GREAT LAKES

abdocorelibrary.com/michigan

HISTORY OF MICHIGAN

Early peoples lived in the Michigan region more than 11,000 years ago. American Indian nations were established in the region by the early 1600s. Major nations included the Potawatomi, Odawa, and Ojibwe. These nations lived in different parts of present-day Michigan. The name Michigan comes from an Ojibwe word meaning "large lake."

This historical depiction shows Ojibwe women gathering wild rice.

EUROPEAN ARRIVAL

French explorers first arrived in the Michigan region in 1622. Many of these explorers were fur traders. Other French settlers included Christian missionaries who worked to spread their religion. A missionary named Jacques Marquette established Sault (pronounced Soo) Sainte Marie in 1668. It was the first French settlement in the Great Lakes region.

The French claimed the area until the French and Indian War (1754–1763). The French and British fought over land. American Indian peoples fought on both sides of the war. The British defeated the French. They won France's land east of the Mississippi River, including present-day Michigan.

Many American Indians were afraid they would lose their land after the British took control. The British had treated American Indian nations poorly during the fur trade. Pontiac, an Odawa leader, led several American Indian nations to attack the British at Fort Detroit in 1763. Other nations involved in Pontiac's War (1763–1766) included the Ojibwe and the Potawatomi. Pontiac was unable to capture Fort Detroit. But Pontiac and his followers did take temporary control over nine forts in the Great Lakes region. Land struggles among American Indian peoples and settlers continued for many years.

THE TREATY OF SAGINAW

In 1819 the Ojibwe signed the Treaty of Saginaw after the War of 1812 (1812–1815). The nation had allied with the British during this war. But after the United States defeated the British, the Ojibwe were left to face American expansion by themselves. The US government forced the Ojibwe to give up more than 4 million acres (1.6 million ha). This was approximately one-third of Michigan's Lower Peninsula.

Michigan remained under British control until the end of the Revolutionary War (1775–1783). The United States won independence from Great Britain as a result of this war. But the British did not give up full control of Michigan until 1796.

An artist depicts Odawa men waiting to attack Fort Detroit during Pontiac's War.

In 1787 the US Congress named the region north of the Ohio River the Northwest Territory. It included modern-day Michigan, Ohio, Indiana, Illinois, Wisconsin, and the eastern part of Minnesota. Over time the US Congress divided the Northwest Territory into smaller territories. The Michigan Territory was created in 1805.

The United States was at war with Great Britain again during the War of 1812 (1812–1815). The British took over Mackinac Island and Detroit for three years. Both sides rushed to build naval power in the Great Lakes. William Henry Harrison led American troops to reclaim Detroit. They pushed the British into Canada.

The war ended when President James Madison signed the Treaty of Ghent. The treaty restored the boundaries that had existed before the war. The US government and the British government also signed the Rush–Bagot Agreement. Both countries got rid of their naval ships on the Great Lakes as part of this agreement. This paved the way for peaceful interactions between the United States and Canada. As of 2021 the agreement is still in effect.

PATH TO STATEHOOD

In the early 1800s there were not many American settlers in the Michigan Territory. That changed after the completion of the Erie Canal in 1825. This made

MICHIGAN
QUICK FACTS

Take a look at Michigan's state symbols. How do they help you understand the state's wildlife?

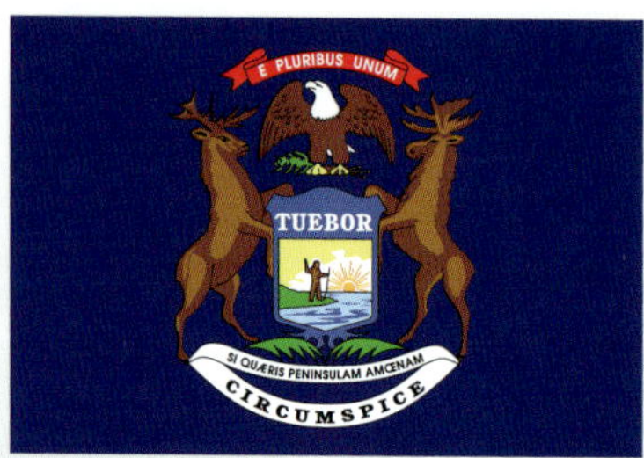

Abbreviation: MI
Nickname: The Great Lakes State
Motto: *Si quaeris peninsulam amoenam, circumspice* (If you seek a pleasant peninsula, look about you)
Date of statehood: January 26, 1837
Capital: Lansing
Population: 10,077,331
Area: 96,714 square miles (250,488 sq km)

STATE SYMBOLS

State bird
American robin

State flower
Apple blossom

State fish
Brook trout

State reptile
Painted turtle

it easier to travel to Michigan from eastern states. American settlers began flooding into the region. This period of population growth was called Michigan Fever.

Michigan created its constitution in 1835. But border disputes with Ohio delayed Michigan's statehood. The states fought over ownership of the Toledo Strip. They both believed the region could serve as a major port city. Michigan did not win the Toledo Strip. In exchange for giving up its claims to the Strip, Michigan received expanded boundaries for the Upper Peninsula. It became the twenty-sixth US state on January 26, 1837.

US states were divided on the issue of slavery. Northern states including Michigan wanted an end to slavery. Southern states wanted to continue the practice. This division led to the American Civil War (1861–1865). Michigan and other Northern states formed the Union. The Union won the war in 1865, and slavery was made illegal throughout the United States.

PERSPECTIVES

FLINT WATER CRISIS

In 2014 state officials changed the city of Flint's water supply in order to save money. Flint residents complained about the new water's smell and taste. The water had high amounts of lead. People can become very sick and even die from lead exposure. It took years for state officials to respond. Most of the population in Flint is Black. A government-appointed report showed that racial discrimination was one reason for the government's slow response. A Flint resident was quoted in the report. The resident said, "If this was in a white area, in a rich area, there would have been something done."

THE GREAT MIGRATION AND UNREST

Factory jobs brought many people to Michigan in the early 1900s. Black people from the South arrived in Michigan to find work and escape discrimination. Between 1915 and 1960, 5 million Black people moved to northern states. This period is called the Great Migration.

But Black people continued to face discrimination in

Michigan. For example, white landlords often refused to rent to Black Americans. Neighborhoods were segregated as a result. In 1943 a fistfight between a Black man and a white man led to widespread violence in Detroit. Black and white Americans looted stores and burned property. At least 34 people were killed during the violence. Many of them were Black.

Violence broke out again in 1967. That year, white police officers raided a Detroit bar that was located in a predominately Black neighborhood. The bar was operating without a license. The officers arrested everyone inside the building. Thousands of people protested the arrests. But the protesters grew violent. Fires and looting occurred throughout the city. The National Guard entered the city to end the unrest. At least 43 people were killed. The five days of civil unrest became known as the Detroit Rebellion. Many white people left the city after the rebellion.

The Michigan State Capitol Building is the state's third capitol building. The first was located in Detroit, and the second was a small wooden building in Lansing.

Racial activism in the community grew. The Michigan and Detroit governments created a program called New Detroit to work toward racial justice. Coleman Young became the first Black mayor of Detroit in 1974. The city worked to employ both Black and white police officers to reduce discrimination. Efforts to reduce discrimination continue today.

GOVERNMENT

Michigan has three branches of government. The legislative branch changes and votes on new and existing laws. The judicial branch is a system of courts. The executive branch includes Michigan's governor, who signs bills into law. There are also 12 federally recognized American Indian tribes in Michigan. Each has its own government that is separate from the state government.

FURTHER EVIDENCE

Chapter Two discusses one of the treaties made between the US government and the American Indian peoples of Michigan. Go to the article below about the 1836 treaty between the US government and the Odawa peoples. Does the information in this article support the point of the chapter? Does it present new evidence?

AUGUSTIN HAMLIN: AN ODAWA WHO HELPED HIS PEOPLE

abdocorelibrary.com/michigan

CHAPTER THREE

GEOGRAPHY AND CLIMATE

Michigan's geography has been shaped over billions of years. Volcanoes erupted in the western UP 2 billion years ago. Layers of lava built up. These layers formed the Porcupine Mountains. This ancient chain of mountains is much smaller today than it was in the past. Glaciers are one reason for this. These massive bodies of ice shaped much of Michigan's geography. Glacial lakes carved step-like formations into the sides of the Porcupine Mountains. Little by little, the

Porcupine Mountains Wilderness State Park is located in the UP. It is the largest state park in Michigan.

Bald eagles hunt in Michigan's Great Lakes.

water washed away pieces of rock. The steps formed over thousands of years. During this time, glaciers also flattened much of the Lower Peninsula.

Glaciers formed the Great Lakes as well as the 11,000 smaller lakes inside the state. These lakes are home to pike, muskies, and sturgeons. Painted turtles are also found in the Great Lakes. This type of turtle has bright colors on its head, legs, and shell. It is Michigan's state reptile.

A number of rivers run through Michigan. Many of them flow into and between the Great Lakes. The Saint Marys River connects Lake Superior to Lake Huron. It serves as the border between the UP and Canada. The Saint Clair River is part of the Great Lakes Waterway. The waterway is made of shipping channels that let cargo ships travel between the Great Lakes.

INVASIVE SPECIES

Invasive species are animals and plants that do not naturally live in a region. Human activities bring them into new areas. Invasive species harm native wildlife. Boats traveling through the Great Lakes are one way that invasive species enter the waters. Zebra mussels are an invasive species in Michigan. They attach to hard surfaces, such as water lines at power plants. This can clog the water lines and increase energy costs. Zebra mussels can even grow on native mussels, killing them.

PERSPECTIVES

ENDANGERED FLOWERS

The dwarf lake iris became the official state wildflower in 1998. This iris grows only on the shores of Lake Michigan and Lake Huron. Its bright blue petals attract bumblebees. These flowers are threatened. People building homes near the lakes destroys the habitat of the flowers. Samantha Nellis is a Michigan scientist. She works to protect the dwarf lake iris. Nellis says that protecting these flowers "helps with clean air and water, which is good for local economies. It's . . . not just about one species—every native species has [a special] quality."

Michigan is home to some rare types of plants and animals. One is a butterfly called Mitchell's satyr. It lives in wetlands in the Lower Peninsula. Another is Michigan's monkey flower. It is found only in a small part of northern Michigan.

CLIMATE

The Great Lakes add moisture to the air, which results in clouds. With only 75 cloudless days each year on average, Michigan is one of the cloudiest US states. In the colder months, the moisture from the Great Lakes

Sections of Lake Superior may freeze during the winter.

creates snowfall. Parts of the UP receive more than 300 inches (762 cm) of snow every year.

With so much snow, only certain plants and animals can survive in Michigan. Paper birches are native to the northern regions of North America, including Michigan. These trees have white bark that reflects sunlight. This allows the trees to maintain a constant temperature during all seasons.

Average yearly rainfall in Michigan is 31 inches (79 cm). Most of the rain falls during the spring and summer. Thunderstorms, tornadoes, and blizzards are common in Michigan. Heavy rains and melting snow can cause floods in early spring.

Extreme weather on the Great Lakes can cause shipwrecks. A storm known as the White Hurricane tore across the Great Lakes in November 1913. Sailors reported heavy snowfall and winds reaching 100 miles per hour (161 km/h). At least eight ships sank during the storm.

STRAIGHT TO THE SOURCE

Alexis de Tocqueville was a French political writer. He traveled to Michigan in 1831. Describing the vast Michigan forests, he wrote:

> *In this ocean of [trees], who can point the way? Where should one direct one's eyes? In vain you climb the tallest trees, only to find yourself surrounded by others still taller. To no avail you climb the hills, for the forest climbs with you everywhere, and this same forest [seems to stretch] from where you stand all the way to the North Pole and the Pacific Ocean.*

Source: John Fierst. "Aristocracy on the Saginaw Trail." *Central Michigan University*, n.d., cmich.edu. Accessed 11 June 2021.

WHAT'S THE BIG IDEA?

Read the passage above carefully. What does it explain about Michigan's forests? Write a sentence stating the main idea. Then write two or three supporting details.

We Can Do

RESOURCES AND ECONOMY

Agriculture plays a large role in Michigan's economy. The Lower Peninsula is home to grasslands. Farmers there raise dairy cows. Michigan is a leading milk-producing state. Michigan farmers also grow fruits such as cherries, apples, and blueberries.

Land in the UP is rich in iron, copper, and other valuable minerals. The Soo Locks and other human-made waterways allowed people to use the Great Lakes to ship these metals and

Rosie the Riveter posters encouraged women to join the workforce during World War II (1939–1945).

minerals to other locations. People mined more copper in the UP between 1845 and 1887 than in any other place in North America. Michigan was also the leader in US iron ore production from the 1850s until the early 1900s. Michigan is still a leading producer of gravel, sand, limestone, salt, nickel, and iron ore.

Michigan's forests are famous for tall white pines and red maple trees. British and American workers used Michigan timber for merchant and war ships. By 1880 Michigan produced as much timber as the next three leading states combined.

NATIONAL CHERRY FESTIVAL

Michigan ranks first in the United States for tart cherry production and fourth for sweet cherries. In 1910 cherry growers started an annual ceremony in May to celebrate the time when the cherry trees blossom. The tradition continued, and today a National Cherry Festival is held every year in Traverse City. In 1987 a world record was set at the festival when workers baked a cherry pie that was 17.5 feet (5 m) wide!

The General Motors Renaissance Center in downtown Detroit serves as the company's headquarters.

MANUFACTURING AND TOURISM

Michigan has many large manufacturing plants near the Great Lakes. The location allows people to easily load products onto huge ships. Michigan is famous for its auto industry. Nearly 20 percent of all vehicles in the United States are made in Michigan. Auto companies General Motors and Ford are headquartered there.

Michigan's identity in the automobile industry was important during World War II (1939–1945). Factories instead began producing weapons, planes, and tanks. Women played a major role in the workforce. Rosie the Riveter became an iconic symbol who encouraged women to help in war efforts. Rose Monroe worked at the Willow Run Bomber Plant in Michigan. She played

Rosie the Riveter in a film.

Today Michigan factories also produce machinery and food products. For example, Kellogg's is a large producer of breakfast cereal and other foods. It is headquartered in Battle Creek.

Tourism is the third-largest industry in Michigan. Lakeshores and forests are popular destinations. Michigan also has many historic mining sites and museums, such as the Detroit Historical Museum.

PERSPECTIVES

HENRY FORD AND THE ASSEMBLY LINE

Henry Ford was a Michigan automobile maker in the 1900s. His famous Model T car became available to the public in 1908. Ford also developed the assembly line. This manufacturing practice made it easy to make many cars in a single day. Ford was able to lower the price of his car, making the Model T available to many more Americans. Nearly half of the cars in the United States in 1918 were Model Ts. Many vehicles and other products today are still made using assembly lines.

STRAIGHT TO THE SOURCE

Henry Ford sold millions of cars and became a world-famous business leader. But before his success, Ford dreamed of creating a car that could be used around the world. He spoke of his goal:

> *I will build a motor car for the great multitude . . . constructed of the best materials, by the best men to be hired, after the simplest designs that modern engineering can devise . . . so low in price that no man making a good salary will be unable to own one and enjoy with his family the blessing of hours of pleasure in God's open spaces."*

Source: "Henry Ford Quotes." *Henry Ford*, 2021, thehenryford.org. Accessed 17 June 2021.

CONSIDER YOUR AUDIENCE

Adapt this quote for a different audience, such as your principal or friends. Write a blog post conveying this same information for the new audience. How does your post differ from the original text and why?

CHAPTER FIVE

PEOPLE AND PLACES

Michigan has a diverse population. White people who are not Hispanic or Latino make up 80 percent of the population. Hispanic and Latino people make up more than 5 percent of Michigan's population. Approximately 14 percent is Black. This percentage is higher in some cities. For example almost 80 percent of Detroit's population is Black. In addition Michigan's population is more than 3 percent Asian and less than 1 percent American Indian.

Stevie Wonder and Marvin Gaye were just two of many Black artists who recorded music at Motown Records in Detroit.

PERSPECTIVES

DIEGO RIVERA

In 1932 Mexican artist Diego Rivera (1886–1957) began to create a series of murals for the Detroit Institute of Arts. It took Rivera nine months to complete 27 paintings on four walls. The murals show Michigan's diverse workers. The paintings include doctors, scientists, and secretaries. Some people are shown working on farmland. The murals also include an image of Henry Ford watching workers on an assembly line. Edsel Ford, Henry Ford's son, praised the murals. He said, "I admire Rivera's spirit. I really believe he was trying to express his idea of the spirit of Detroit."

MICHIGAN ATTRACTIONS

There is much to see and do in Michigan cities. The Lower Peninsula has many museums and sports venues. The Detroit Institute of Arts is a world-famous art museum. People can tour the museum. They can also attend drawing classes or watch movies. The scenic UP has many state parks. Tahquamenon Falls State Park in Paradise features waterfalls and hiking paths. The UP is also home to the Ottawa National Forest and the Hiawatha National Forest, which cover nearly 2 million acres (0.8 million ha).

Berry Gordy was born in Detroit in 1929. He founded Motown Records in 1959, which led to a new era for Black musicians. Pop, soul, and funk music streamed out of the studio. Gordy encouraged artists such as the Temptations and the Jackson 5 to make their own sounds. At the time, radio stations were segregated. Different stations appealed to Black or white audiences. Motown songs were some of the first to achieve crossover success. Songs by Black musicians played on white radio stations. Today Gordy's legacy is celebrated at the Motown Museum in Detroit. It is located at the original headquarters and recording studio.

Detroit is also home to the state's major professional sports teams. These teams are the Tigers, Lions, Red Wings, and Pistons. College sports are

University of Michigan football fans cheered on the Wolverines during a game against the Nebraska Cornhuskers in 2018.

huge in Michigan too. For example, the University of Michigan Wolverines play football at Michigan Stadium in Ann Arbor. It is the largest football stadium in the United States. It can hold more than 107,000 people.

Visitors to Michigan can learn about auto manufacturing. They can hike in forests in the Upper

Holland, Michigan, hosts the Tulip Time Festival each year.

Peninsula and surf on Lake Superior. They can enjoy local cherries at state festivals and learn about Michigan culture at museums. With its interesting history, beautiful scenery, and important industries, Michigan has something for everyone.

THE WOLVERINE STATE

Michigan is sometimes called the Wolverine State. But wolverines are extremely rare in Michigan. The wolverine is the largest member of the weasel family. It is known for being stubborn, mean, and prone to fighting. Some historians think that the nickname comes from the Toledo Strip border dispute between Michigan and Ohio. Because the fighters from Michigan were fierce and persistent, they earned the nickname Wolverines.

IMPORTANT DATES

11,000 years ago
Early peoples live in the Michigan region.

1622
French explorers arrive in Michigan.

1668
Jacques Marquette establishes the first French settlement in the Great Lakes region at Sault Sainte Marie.

1763
Odawa leader Pontiac leads American Indian nations to attack British forts throughout the Great Lakes region.

1805
The US Congress creates the Michigan Territory.

1837
Michigan becomes the twenty-sixth state on January 26.

1913

The White Hurricane strikes the Great Lakes region.

1967

People protest arrests that occurred in a predominantly Black neighborhood of Detroit. Protests during the Detroit Rebellion grow violent.

2014

State officials change the water supply in Flint. The new water source contains high amounts of lead, resulting in the Flint water crisis.

STOP AND THINK

Another View

This book talks about the Great Lakes. As you know, every source is different. Ask a librarian or another adult to help you find another source about the Great Lakes. Write a short essay comparing and contrasting the new source's point of view with that of this book's author. What is the point of view of each author? How are they similar and why? How are they different and why?

Dig Deeper

After reading this book, what questions do you still have about Michigan? With an adult's help, find a few reliable sources that can help you answer your questions. Write a paragraph about what you learned.

Tell the Tale

Chapter One of this book discusses a visitor's first impression of Mackinac Island. Imagine you are visiting the island. Write 200 words about your visit. Describe how you got to the island and what you saw there. How is the island special? What is its historical importance?

Surprise Me

Chapter Two describes some important events in the history of Michigan. After reading this book, what two or three facts about the history of Michigan did you find most surprising? Write a few sentences about each fact. Why did you find each fact surprising?

GLOSSARY

activism
the process of taking action to make social or political changes

assembly line
a manufacturing process in which a series of machines and workers perform specific tasks to complete a product

canal
a long, human-made ditch that allows water to flow from one area to another

civil unrest
violent activity that arises from a social demonstration

discrimination
when people treat others differently based on certain factors such as appearance

glacier
a large body of ice that moves across land

habitat
the place where a plant or an animal lives

peninsula
a body of land that is surrounded by water on three sides

treaty
an official agreement between governments

ONLINE RESOURCES

To learn more about Michigan, visit our free resource websites below.

Visit **abdocorelibrary.com** or scan this QR code for free Common Core resources for teachers and students, including vetted activities, multimedia, and booklinks, for deeper subject comprehension.

Visit **abdobooklinks.com** or scan this QR code for free additional online weblinks for further learning. These links are routinely monitored and updated to provide the most current information available.

LEARN MORE

Banting, Erinn. *Lake Michigan*. Lightbox, 2020.

Isgro, Bailey Sisoy. *Rosie, a Detroit Herstory*. Wayne State University, 2018.

INDEX

About the Author

Jane Vernon is the author of more than 100 books for children, both nonfiction and fiction. Her favorite topics are nature; arts and crafts; food and cooking; biographies; health; survival; and science, technology, engineering, and math (STEM). Jane and her husband live on the central coast of California.